PEPPERMINT
DREAMS

PEPPERMINT DREAMS

·

LINDA WILKINSON

HARVEST HOUSE PUBLISHERS
Irvine, California 92714

PEPPERMINT DREAMS

© 1977 by Harvest House Publishers
Irvine, California 92714

Library of Congress Catalog Card Number; 77-81667
ISBN: 0-89081-070-2

Printed in the United States of America

Design and Photos; Koechel Design, Minneapolis

CONTENTS

THE HUNGRY ONES

Drifting in and out of daydreams
with visions of my God —
I am one of the hungry ones,
never quite full to the top ones.
Lord give me the pieces and maybe
with the aid of your hands
we can put them together
to fit the mold you had planned.
You gave me a reason to shout with joy —
you gave me the love, the vision —
a sense of feeling for your people —
to live beyond the problems,
to live above the hurt,
untouched by the masses —
willing to give up my very last shirt.
Is this your calling — to give me a song,
to never be quite full—always asking for more
so I can give love
even when the rich are becoming so poor.

Are the pieces slowly falling into place —
do they need a shove
to fit into that tight space —
I don't think I can make it Lord —
at least not on my own —
for just about the time I've got it together,
the table is tipped
and the pieces fall to the floor.
Oh please one more chance —
for the life that you've promised —
one more minute to be filled with joy,
to laugh or to cry —
just to feel.
Don't ever let me be full God,
then I could not ask for more —
always a bit hungry, always a bit tired—
Lord, if I were perfect
the world could not contain my joy.

Did you say that I am the salt of the earth —
could that be the richness coming from blessings
that only God could supply—or is it my imagination
as lucid as a bird in the sky.
I don't know all your ways Lord —
but then I don't have to try.
I don't have to think beyond this day —
look beyond this night,
or hope to grasp fruit—that is
not yet even ripe.

SEASONED
BLESSINGS

You're still striving to put me together,
to mold my body and soul —
to weld my conscious mind to where living waters flow.
you're building an empire in my heart to contain
a throne for which only Christ will have a part.
I'm longing to see the finished product
as it emerges from your side —
as it becomes more substantial than water
and more rampant than a raging tide.
As this is taking place you're patiently
holding my head high —
and lifting my spirits to soar way beyond your sky.
And yet, you're allowing me to be seasoned
with the salt of the earth —
to use it for blessing—no matter what my worth.
Was the seasoning added in the beginning
or was it a gift from your Son —
for I am created as He was—and I can sense
that He must have had some.
A bit of salt in His life—just as there is in mine —
to lend some flavor when the fruit is bitter —
and yet coming off the vine.

A CARING MIND

The strength and compassion
of a caring mind
can still a thousand worries and
release eyes made blind.
Caring minds open valleys of thoughts and fears —
turn them into peaks of nurtured wisdom —
and dreams beyond their years.
Someone with a caring heart can
reopen a land of promise
once thought dormant and dry —
and turn it into a field of thriving blossoms
reaching up to the sky.
I have been that person
in need of a caring soul
to simply unblock the arteries
and let the blessing flow.
I took much effort and a little pain
to be so patient and yet try
to explain the reason for His insistence
that I was not to faint —
but take another step
no matter what my complaint.
The valleys do not seem so low,
nor the mountaintops so high —
for my footsteps have been led
by the one with a caring mind.

PEPPERMINT DREAMS

Strawberry balloons
and peach colored moons,
grapefruit skies and blueberry pies,
favorite surprises popping into view —
looks of delight from people like you.
Friends and children,
bubble gum and flowers —
going hand in hand with happiness
and showers.
This is life and this is breath
of whispering promises given until death.
Hold on to their hope, caress their existence —
they were given to bring smiles
in hearts of dependence.
Hearts that rely on the promise of youth,
hearts that believe in sentiment and truth.
People who fly on peppermint clouds
can lighten the hearts of strangers in crowds.
Thank goodness for dreamers
and frivolous minds
and thank you dear Lord
for the love that they find.

Blanketed miracles lie beneath
the grain of a bushel yet unharvested.
Bit by bit the pieces fall into place,
the hearts soften—people listen.
Strange and unbelievable the air that I breathe —
for lying within it is one particular seed.
A fantasy of glamour—a quick dash of joy
seasoned with love—baked in a kettle
yet untouched and never quite settled.
It is steaming and brewing but never quite done,
for the ingredients are rare and lacking just one.
It could be the spice, the blessing or the cause —
but until it's well stirred it's life without a reason.

GOD'S
SOUFFLE

It's death looking downward in the flame of a neon sign —
a glow of impatience—a spirited mind.
The finished product is like a souffle —
proud and perfect until cut by human hands,
but the taste is pleasant even though
the imperfections had to be planned.
There was no other way to get to the core
but to cut the surface—let out the air —
then to partake of what was laying in there.
Given a chance to be digested and enjoyed
is maybe the greatest blessing of living —
bringing food to the hungry mind is a
special way of seasoning —
lives needing a cause and a reason for existing.

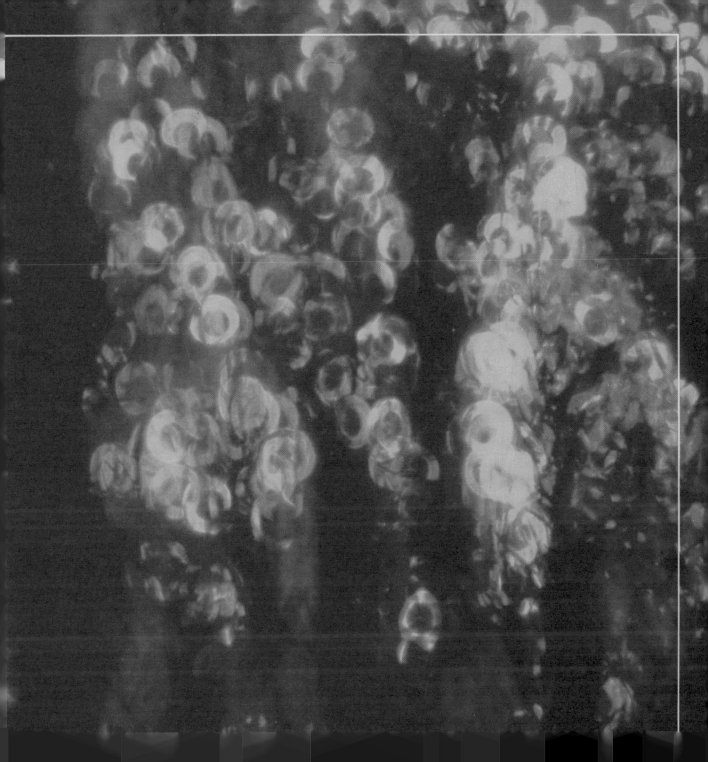

Lord, I didn't see your creation
until I held it in the palm of my hand.
I didn't understand your ways
until before a thousand people I had to take a stand.
I didn't hear your voice
until my heart was broken because there was no other choice.
Faith in you was never possible until my
feet were sinking in sand
and then dear God I felt your hand.
Bending down you picked me up,
brushing away the dirt and soil —
smiling—you gave me a reason to thank you
for those days of fear and toil.
You loved me through it all—you cared
when I was too ashamed to call.

You didn't ridicule, you didn't shout —
you just very carefully lifted me out.
Out of a prison of greying white
into new dimensions beyond my sight.
Thank you dear God for letting me be human
and for helping me to understand —
the imperfections in your children
when they forget to take your hand.
You knew I had been there—groping for my way.
You knew I could be trusted
to show your little ones the way.
Thank you dear God for believing in me
and for giving me strength to tell the world
I am free.

BETWEEN THE CLOUDS

The daisies didn't come today —
but that's alright,
there's a field of them just outside the door.
Those promises didn't come to pass —
but what is that,
they might only have been made of glass.
The sun didn't shine on my day —
but rain was needed anyway.
Your heart was not receptive to mine
when I thought it should have been —
but by tomorrow a greater fortune may lie therein.

The song I hear is not the one I asked for —
but if I listen carefully —
I may like this one even more.
Can you imagine my tomorrow —
daisies blowing in the wind,
promises being kept,
sun shining without a cloud
and your heart waiting for mine —
to share the song I heard and the lesson I gained
while walking in the rain.

Thankfulness is now pouring from my heart —
but once —
I looked unto the mountains and
I looked into the sea.
I looked under my daydreams and
I found only me.
I had foolishly squandered a piece of my soul —
lost in a game that was a joy to behold.
A joy for a second—becoming disaster —
dying before I could hear my own laughter.
So careful and tenderly the piece had to be found —
the piece that was laying on unhallowed ground.
It had to be cared for —
fed with love, nurtured with joy.
It had needed a reason to once again live —
to re-enter the kingdom that promises life.
It is now living so richly
as on the mountaintop it stands —
and the sea is now calm as I'm sifting the sand.

A PIECE
OF SOUL

Realities are precious —
they happen so easily, without any schemes.
Much better than hoped for in any of my dreams.
I'm recapturing the treasures
that had been thrown away.
I'm guarding them with life
as I'm re-entering the fold.
You kept your promise Lord —
a better shepherd there never could be.
My soul is complete —
the piece that was missing
turned up at your feet.

Butterflies and buttonwillows —
a freedom of mind
from cobwebs and crawdads
that so often make me blind.
A time for planting seeds
into a furrowed brain,
that became delirious
from too much heat and pain.

BUTTERFLIES AND BUTTONWILLOWS

So fresh the blessings of a baby flower
once the seed of a buttonwillow
now holding a greater power.
The new birth it has been given
could remove all the pain
from tear stained eyes
along the pathway to my brain.
Butterflies and Buttonwillows
our very dearest friends,
bring spiritual awakening
and tenderness of heart.

Carousels filled with animals of unusual kinds —
keeping time to the music
for children waiting in line.
They ask nothing of their passengers —
they need no other joy,
than the laughter and contentment of each girl and boy.
Drifting in and out of songs —
heard by many generations —
the message remains the same
for the children of God's creation.
He knew there would be times
when boredom and doubt would cloud our minds.
If only we would stop and listen for the music
if only we would wish a little harder for the golden ring —
it's time to find a friend and jump on board —
for the music doesn't stop for long —
just time enough for us to climb on.
They're moving now —
those animals of red and gold and blue —
their journey won't be far —
in hopes of bringing you —
a very special joy that somehow seemed impossible to find.
Don't be impatient and don't jump off the side —
there will be another song each time that you ride.

LOVING

Loving uncomplicated objects of affection
is so easily done —
while loving the unlovely is not quite so much fun.
Stretching my heart to hold the needs of your love —
is a bit more than expected, leaving me unprotected.
I find that the risk is greater in giving
for I have no way of knowing just what you are feeling.
Are you going to be kind and patient —
giving me your best,
or are you going to handle my love
lightly—putting me to the test?
Are you going to demand of me
or are you going to feed my soul
with flattery and flowers?
Are you going to fit the role?
It's another chance I take —
hoping for charity from you,
I still sometimes
wonder if your motives are true.
You see I cannot explain love
or paint you a picture —
I don't even understand my deepest desire
for just about the time I'm feeling close to hate,
a warm blanket of love again is my fate.
As it is taking over and enfolding my heart —
I know I've allowed love its rightful part.

SALT OF MY SPIRIT

Lifted out of your spirit and into mine —
the spray of the salt
is the frosting from my mind.
The splash of the waves
is my cleansing lotion —
many lives it has saved when out of the notion.
The grit and the brine are just a sample
from the creatures of the deep —
they helped you to believe that I am creation
and I am your strength.
For nothing could be so powerful as a conjugated wave,
put together by my handiwork,
freeing you from being a slave.

The breathing in of its vapors
is like feeling the breath of God —
nothing is so invigorating or so tantalizing
as long as you're moving with the tide —
your boat is on course, your life in its glide.
The taste of the salt that is left on your lips
is a pleasant reminder that I'm in charge of your ship.
The movement of your body as you merge with the waves
is your assurance of my presence—it never betrays.
Drink in the salt of the spirited sea
and take it to the people who are longing for me.

I didn't ask if I could be your friend —
I didn't stop to question if an hour
was too long to spend.
I didn't stop to think
if my call interrupted your day —
I only wanted some answers
when I was too down to pray.
I didn't stop to analyze
what might have been happening in your mind —
I didn't think to remember
that today was your day to unwind.
I don't always think of reasons
to ask for your time —
I don't have any motive
than just to be in tune with your mind.

It might be important to use the hour for fun.
To love without cause or reason —
to know that we don't have to run.
To believe that it's special just being alive
with no heavy discussions on what's happening in life.
Could you do all this without feeling guilty
or do you have to go on with your schedule,
you'll live and be happy—
but never completely know the joy —
because you didn't take time to be human,
didn't have time for fun —
always needing a reason for the hour
that was to be the prize I had won.

Out of desperation I walked into your house —
I listened to your guests,
I learned how your children love you
and obey your command.
I even heard them saying they could feel the guidance of your hand.
I did not wonder if what they said was true,
because out of desperation I wanted to be closer to you.
I played into their game Lord,
or so it seemed —
I found I had been accepted —
I gave to the poor and I counseled the depressed,
I loved the ones who were hurt
and clothed the souls that were undressed.
As I was helping to spread this good news —
I felt my desperation would diminish
and I would definitely get rid of this knowing exasperation

DESPERATION

And then as I sat quietly hoping to hear your voice —
I heard a sound—the feet of a stranger approaching.
As I looked I realized his philosophy was different —
his life not understood.
I wondered as he came closer
if I should take his hand —
or just let him walk on by,
knowing that we didn't understand.
Could he feel the pain that I felt,
even though I followed all the rules,
did what all the people said to do,
and went to all the right schools.
After all I was easily accepted among my group —
I honestly believed I could trust these people —
their sign of the fish was living proof.

Oh Lord, my faith has been shaken—
I seem to have lost my trust —
I did exactly as your guests did,
I felt it was a must.
Just run me through one more time Lord —
I've learned that you're my example.

The shadow on the wall of a broken dream
is just a memory of a well thought scheme
to obtain the impossible.
Rely on God—for all His strength
is all that is needed
to piece together a life depleted.
Look to this life of quiet rest
with full dependence on God
who upon you has blessed.
It is His decision
to make you into a statue of wax and gold —
easily molded but not so easily sold.
For you could not be bought
for any price by any man.
A piece of freedom
is your's through Jesus Christ —
you have only to take His hand.

A PIECE
OF FREEDOM

Why isn't my nature more problem free?
Did I plan on making a fool out of me?
A clever potter who took His hands
and created the life that before you stands.
He didn't make me from the angels dust —
I'm made of clay—I forget how to trust.
Sometimes I crumble and fill the room with fear,
because of my nature I'm not always of good cheer.

my
ASSURANCE

I'll try a bit harder to be problem free —
but I'm afraid I didn't come with a limited guarantee.
The world is not perfect nor is my body of clay,
but give me a chance—I might bring joy to your day.
For nowhere can I find that my Lord did reveal
that Life would be free of problems —
He just promised to heal —
the sins and the hurt,
the doubts and the fears —
the flaws in my nature are covered with His tears.
That's the only security that came along with me,
a policy of forgiveness —
His assurance is free.

I am reaping the harvest of the golden grain,
but may my eyes always be stayed on you Lord —
from which this valued gift came.
May I always see the good
in the children you call your own.
May their minds profit from the fortune
laying before your throne.
As you help to show me your infinite ways
of turning lives into miracles —
may I not forget to praise —
for unless I remember to give the thanks to you,
I then have lost the vision of the only solid truth.
You'll never be finished feeding my soul
from the wheat of your harvest,
from the grain that is gold.
The empty kernels are not good enough,
though they're easier to find —
they do not fill an empty stomach
or nurture a frozen mind.
Give me the joy of showing your children
how to plant the grain,
give me your peace and help me try to explain —
that their house can be full of plenty,
their lives a miracle a day —
if they can remember what you've done —
the fruit of your harvest
was the gift of your Son.

THE
HARVEST
FROM
YOUR
HOUSE

JOY

My product of joy is unselfishness
towards other human beings
existing in my life.
It could be an illusion in my mind —
but when I see warm human smiles
I know it will be impossible to find sadness.
I can look a floppy Raggedy Ann in the eye
and discover more Joy
than I could ever get in anything I would buy.

I feel joy when I reach out
and hold the spray from the ocean in my hands —
and I think of a thousand miracles
to bring peace to many lands —
but it all comes back to joy.
The root of all goodness
is a look into a heart filled with sadness —
only then do you find the strength
you've been promised to bring gladness.
And maybe tomorrow when I walk by the sea —
I will solve the world's problems,
my Raggedy Ann and me —
and it all comes back to joy.
Unable to live in a world of grief —
joy is the most pleasant relief.

THE MASTER PLAN

I have been part of the Master's plan
in achieving the goals set forth on this land.
However, I cannot take the credit
for the fruit growing here—for without the blueprint of the Master
I would have evaporated into fear.
The diagrams seen on paper
look so complicated to the naked eye,
but in the mind of the Master are so simplified.
The beauty of the finished drawing
never shows all the lines —
or the smudges of the ink,
it only reveals a careful design. And as I unroll the final picture —
it is so very clear that what I see now
could have only been drawn by the Master's hand—
as he set forth to lay out His plan.

CELEBRATION

I want to celebrate living,
give of the joy that you're giving.
Oh Lord of mine I had no idea
that the sky could look so blue,
that the earth could be so alive,
that I could look directly at you.
The promise of life beyond death
just makes me want to go on living —

to digest the abundance from the honey of the bees,
to gaze upon each tiny leaf falling from your trees.
Life hereafter must be unthinkably glorious —
because to me life here on earth
has contained moments that were joyous.
One tiny second without your love,
I would have blown out like a candle,
I would have been snuffed out like a flame —
but you've kept me burning
with enough light to see
that I can celebrate living
no matter what ever happens to me.

WHY TOMORROW LORD

Why tomorrow
when I could have made a success of today.
Why did I put off doing what I had to do —
why did I give in to the character I play.
Did I feel life was too short
to miss one tiny minute,
therefore jeopardizing my soul
and pushing it to the limit.
Well, I gained a fortune of loose ended lies
and much to no ones surprise —
I'm crying why tomorrow
when I could have made use of today.
This episode has ended
will there be another —
after all I'm vulnerable to just being alive,
how will I ever survive —
and when I wake in the morning —
it will be tomorrow.
If you'll give me your strength,
I'll give you my sorrow —
and I promise I won't ask why.

A gift of honor given out of love —
or was it a bribe for me to deliver
what you felt I had plenty of.
Can you give freely or is it necessary for you to believe
that the receiver reciprocate
or you'll go and retrieve —
the gift that was given supposedly from love.
And then you found your heart was thickening
to the needs and desires of your fellow man,
for after all who were you
to generously lift a hand. I believe God understands you —
He knows it's hard to give up
that which was difficult to obtain,
but He'll bless you ten fold if you'll just not refrain—
from giving freely and not expect the reward
to come from an earthly source.
For He is the giver of all good gifts,
if you've chosen wisely in your course.
I'm sure you know
that love is the greatest gift of all —
but given without honor it will surely fall.

A
GIFT
OF
HONOR